TEEN
STRESS

D1522025

TEEN STRESS

STORIES TO GUIDE YOU

William L. Coleman

Augsburg

MINNEAPOLIS

TEEN STRESS
Stories to Guide You

Cover Design and Cover Illustration: John P. Hanson

Library of Congress Cataloging-in-Publication Data

Coleman, William L.
    Teen stress : stories to guide you / William Coleman.
      p.   cm.
    ISBN 0-8066-2732-8 (alk. paper)
    1. Teenagers—Prayer-books and devotions—English. 2. Stress in adolescence—Religious aspects—Christianity—Prayer-books and devotions—English. [1. Conduct of life. 2. Christian life.]
I. Title.
BV4850.C5656   1994
248.8'3—dc20   94-33427
                                                CIP
                                                AC

The paper used in this publication meets the minimum requirements of American National Standard for Information Sciences—Permanence of Paper for Printed Library Materials, ANSI Z329.48—1984. ∞™

Manufactured in the U.S.A.   AF 9-2732

98 97 96   2 3 4 5 6 7 8 9 10

Contents

When Your Hair Stands on End
(A Note to the Reader)

Have you ever been outside and felt the hair on the back of your neck start to rise? If you have, you had better hit the ground. There's a good chance lightning could strike you!

If you're a teen, it seems like hair is continuously rising on the back of your neck. Pressure, stress, and tension are often in the air around you and your friends. School, home, the streets, stadiums, parties, and contests are all places and events where stress can be terrible.

There may be no age group that suffers from more stress than you do as a teen. I believe God knows that and God would like to help you.

BILL COLEMAN

Thanks!

They always come through. Teens from all over the country have told me how they feel about pressure and what they do about it. From South Carolina, Michigan, Kansas, Nebraska, and other states they have explained what goes on in the world where they live.

I can't name everyone who helped but I particularly want to express my gratitude to "The Group." They have opened up again and given me an education.

Jana Breese	Stephanie Klein
Le Bouatick	Aaron Oswald
Loli Bouatick	Chad Oswald
Donald Gimpel	Jeff Pritner
Justin Gimpel	Chris Widga
Charlie Janzen	Kevin Widga

Any stories I have used have been changed enough to camouflage their sources. However, the principles I learned from teens are very prominent in the book.

Good Things Happen

"Blessing" is a church word. We seldom use it anyplace else. If someone gives you a ride home after school, you probably don't say, "Bless you." You don't tell a waitress "Bless you" when she brings the pizza. Who wants to get laughed out of the place?

But even if it is a peculiar Bible/church word, blessings do happen. The word blessing simply means that God has done something good for us. Whatever word we use for it, the fact remains the same; God sends good things our way every day, whether we recognize them or not.

If you listen to someone grump, you would think that nothing good had ever happened to him. He bad-mouths everything. According to him nothing works; nothing gets better; no one is kind; there's no sense in getting up for tomorrow. Most of us have some days like this. Some of us bad-mouth for weeks or even months.

Living would be tough if good things never happen. Can you imagine 365 days of everything falling apart? If each day is a bummer, it's a wonder we don't fall apart.

In order to be fair to ourselves and fair to God, we need to make a short list of good things. Write them down. Name just three good things that have happened to you. (You can call them three ways that God has blessed you, but if that sounds too religious for you, that's okay.)

It's hard to write down three things if you think life is ugly and rotten, but try. This is the first step to admitting that there is a ray of sunshine some-place. Most people who make this list will feel better right away. They have recognized the fact that life has some good things to offer and that a few of those good things have come their way.

After we accept the fact that we have something good, we will soon be able to thank God for the blessings . . . oops . . . the good things we have received.

Good things are going on as surely as bad things are going on. The trick is to concentrate on the good ones.

"You will be blessed when you come in and blessed when you go out."
Deuteronomy 28:6

Keep thinking

1. Name one good thing in your life.
2. Name a second good thing in your life.
3. Name a third good thing in your life.

Pressure from Friends

A police officer who works regularly with teen-agers said their pressure from friends is enormous. "When I was young," he said, "the pressure came from having pimples and being overweight, but to-day the pressure is too great."

Everyone wants to feel accepted and wanted, but our search for friends can get us into more trouble than we ever dreamed.

Friends are like life jackets. If you put them on correctly, they will keep your head out of the water and help you survive. But if life jackets are tied on backwards, they can actually hold your face and head under the water and drown you.

Hanging out with the wrong crowd causes many teenagers to do foolish, even disastrous, things. When we read about two young people getting into trouble, we often wonder if one would have done it without the other. Did one of them make a mistake of spending too much time with the wrong person?

How many teenagers were introduced to drugs by friends? Probably only a few got their first drugs from enemies or strangers. Someone they knew said, "Try it. It won't hurt you." It's hard to turn down a friend. We don't want to disappoint anyone. We don't want anyone to think we are afraid or that we won't go along. Young people are far more likely to try something if their friends put the pressure on.

Once we have a friend, it's hard to change. A friend is someone we like. We have good times and a lot of laughs together. It's hard to say "That's enough. We aren't going to hang out together anymore."

But, once in a while, we have to take inventory of our friends. It's like checking over a bag of apples. If one apple is rotten, before long the other apples will go bad also. The rotten apple has to be removed before it destroys the entire bag.

No one makes that choice easily. Some of us never do make that decision and we end up getting hurt.

Open your hand and spread your fingers out. Give each finger and your thumb the name of a friend. Now ask yourself, "Is one of my friends dragging me down? Is there someone who pressures me into doing things that will lead to trouble?"

Is there a friend you need to move away from and other friends you need to move closer to? Maybe you need to ask God to help you make that decision.

"A righteous man is cautious in friendship,
but the way of the wicked leads them astray."
Proverbs 12:26

Keep thinking

1. Do you feel pressure from a friend to do something you think is wrong?
2. Do you have a friend who is a bad influence?
3. Is there another friend you would like to move closer to? Who?

The Competition for Grades

Is your teacher giving you that look? Are her eyes shooting darts in your direction? Is her jaw set like stone? Does her wrinkled frown send a silent message? Is she letting you know that your grades are heading south?

After your parent looked at your report card, did he or she suggest you apply for dog-grooming school? Was your allowance cut to a nickel? Did your parent sit silently at the table, tight-lipped except for an occasional, "Well, well"?

Are you working harder to get good grades but enjoying it less? Do you feel the crunch? Would you like to throw your books away and seek a career as a surfer?

The tension to get good grades has a way of getting out of hand. Eventually almost everyone becomes nervous, anxious, and jittery. Around exam time some students go to bed and simply stay there, too frightened to attend classes. Others stay up all night and eat junk food until they can't think anymore. Too many become so scared that they cheat or even get someone else to take tests for them.

Before tension tears you apart, consider four easy steps to lower your blood pressure and calm down your sweat glands.

1. *Tell yourself it is all right if you fail.* God will still love you, the birds will still sing, the Mississippi

will still flow, and you can still order a burger and fries. You aren't likely to fail, but even if you do, God is in control and life will go on.

2. *Study a reasonable amount.* The two big mistakes are: (1) don't study at all and hope you luck out or (2) study until you can't think. Give the books a strong, honest shot and then put them to bed.

3. *Eat real food.* Too much junk food and sugar can send you way up and then send you crashing down. A well-balanced meal may sound boring, but it could keep you relaxed.

4. *Mix it with some exercise.* Walks, sit-ups, or a little racquetball help lower the tension and wake up the brain. Sitting in one position for hours tends to leave everything numb.

God must worry about students who go bonkers chasing grades. They have lost their joy.

It sounds like whoever wrote Ecclesiastes probably took a history exam:

> *"Of making many books there is no end, and much study wearies the body."*
>
> *(12:12)*

Keep thinking

1. Who gets on your case the most about grades? Teachers, parents, yourself? Why?
2. Do you think people who get C's aren't as good as people who get A's?
3. Which is more important: good health or good grades?

Boundaries Are Important

Try to imagine a world without boundaries. Without shorelines and riverbanks, the entire earth would be covered with water. If we didn't have walls and roofs the wind would whistle through our living rooms and rain would pound into our bedrooms. If the earth itself ran outside its orbit, we would freeze as the planet went farther from the sun and melt as it drew closer.

Boundaries aren't bad. If nature threw off its restrictions, our lives would become unbearable.

Teens often gripe about boundaries. They don't like it when parents place limits on their activities. That's one of the reasons why we hear so many complaints about curfews.

Most young people still have curfews. And the majority of those teens still complain. If you listen, you might think they want no nighttime restrictions at all. But when you start to ask questions, you hear them say something else.

For most teens (but not all) the lack of curfews would bring chaos, uncertainty, and tremendous stress. They would prefer some limits rather than try and figure out the rules every evening and every weekend.

Without boundaries:

Teens feel uneasy.

Parents worry.

Young people have trouble drawing limits.

Situations are riskier late at night.

Pressures are harder to handle.

Teens see curfews as signs that their parents care. With so many other decisions to make, curfews might help reduce tension.

We all know some young people with no curfew, and that may work great for them. They set their own boundaries and keep them. But most teens seem to function better if parents help establish a few borders.

Eventually everyone must work out his own limits, but as we wiggle into adulthood we untie the ropes a little at a time. Never curse the boundaries that actually might be a big help.

God set the world in order with dependable barriers. Sometimes they are shaken, but usually they hold. All of God's creation functions better with restraints.

> *"I made the sand a boundary for the sea, an everlasting barrier it cannot cross. The waves may roll, but they cannot prevail; they may roar, but they cannot cross it."*
>
> *Jeremiah 5:22*

Keep thinking

1. Do you function better with or without a curfew?
2. What limits do your parents set that you appreciate?

Sports Stress

For millions of teenagers organized sports have become filled with too much tension to be fun. Many were pushed or prodded into playing team sports when they were as young as five years old. Someone placed a ball on a tee and invited the kid to smack a home run. She or he obediently played this or some other game for the next seven years and then began to tire of the stress.

With so much emphasis on organized sports, teenagers are often torn apart by the pressure. Either their parents or their friends or their coaches get on their cases and try to force them to join a team. If they don't join something, they often feel guilty or chicken or like some kind of lowlife.

By the time they become middle teenagers the great majority of young people no longer participate in team sports, either in school or any other place. According to a study at Michigan State University, the five leading reasons why teens drop out of organized sports are:

> They lose interest.
> It isn't any fun.
> It takes too much time.
> Coach isn't a good teacher.
> It's too much pressure.

Organized sports is a terrific idea for many teens, but it definitely isn't for everyone. The bad thing is that too many people feel useless the rest of their lives because they didn't pursue athletics.

Athletics is just a small part of life. Never feel it's the most important thing people do. God didn't say that life's purpose is to see how far we can throw a ball.

If we don't like organized sports or don't feel like we fit, there is still hope. All of us can participate in some reasonable form of recreation. We can run, walk, throw frisbees, play backyard football, or just get active. Exercise helps us relax, wakes up our brains, takes a couple of pounds off, and might put a little color in our cheeks. Athletics should help us cut stress, not increase it.

There are more important things than athletics. Two thousand years ago the apostle Paul wrote that godliness is of greater value than exercise. Sports are a good part of life but hardly the whole enchilada. Keep everything in its right perspective.

"For physical training is of some value, but godliness has value for all things, holding promise for both the present life and the life to come."

1 Timothy 4:8

Keep thinking

1. What's your favorite form of exercise?
2. Do you tend to think of yourself as active or inactive?
3. Which exercise leaves you relaxed?

A Bothered Conscience

There was a girl in the tenth grade at Logan High who was teased mercilessly. Her hair was never right and her clothes were out-of-date. They looked handed down from an older sister.

The girl's grades weren't much and she didn't belong to any extra activity. Behind her back the other students called her names like Granny, Retardo, and a few we can't print. Seldom did they call her by her real name.

At the end of the semester she turned sixteen and dropped out of school. No one ever saw her again and they wondered if she had moved away.

Two weeks before school was to begin in the fall, Jamie stopped to see Lisa, the sponsor of her youth group at church.

"I feel terrible about the way I treated her," Jamie explained as they sat on the porch steps.

"It doesn't sound very pretty," Lisa agreed.

"My friends tell me not to feel guilty. After all, everybody did it. But I do feel guilty."

"I wouldn't argue with you, Jamie." Lisa looked her in the eye. "You sound guilty to me. All of us do rotten things to people."

"You do understand, don't you?" Jamie's voice rose. "People try to convince me that it wasn't so bad. But it was."

"It doesn't help to pretend when inside we know we did something wrong."

"Exactly."

"That's great when we can admit our mistakes," Lisa continued.

"What do I do now?" Jamie wondered.

"There are a couple of things you might do. If you know where she lives, you could go and apologize. Another thing is to promise yourself that you will never again treat anyone else that way."

"Oh, I wouldn't," Jamie insisted. "It was a terrible thing to do."

"I think God understands," Lisa said earnestly. "Sometimes we are guilty and we need to do something about it. God's in the business of forgiving guilty people."

"Let us draw near to God with a sincere heart in full assurance of faith, having our hearts sprinkled to cleanse us from a guilty conscience and having our bodies washed with pure water."

Hebrews 10:22

Keep thinking

1. Do you feel tension because of something you know you did wrong?
2. Is there someone you should tell?
3. Have you explained to God what you did?

Parents at War

Have you ever felt like the room was filled with tension? No one is shouting or arguing; in fact, no one is saying anything and yet you can sense the electricity in the air.

That's what Katie picked up one autumn evening at her house. Her father didn't eat with the family but instead drifted out into the garage. He was probably checking the oil in his car. Katie's mother ate with her but barely said a word.

After they finished eating, Mom went into the kitchen while Katie shuffled sadly toward the family room. She didn't have to be a private investigator to figure this one out. Her parents were on the fritz.

But why? Were they angry at each other? Did somebody die? Were they mad at her? Did someone lose his job? Katie wanted to pull her hair and scream, "What in the world is going on around here?"

Teens have their own built-in Richter scales. They can tell when there are slight tremors rattling through the house. They can usually read whether it's a major earthquake or simply some minor shake.

But most of us have trouble figuring out what caused the family to rumble. Who did what? Who said what? What's happening now? Often there is only one way to find those answers. We have to ask.

Katie stopped pulling her hair, biting her lip, and trembling. She walked into the kitchen, put her hand on her mother's shoulder and said, "I'd appreciate it if you'd tell me what's going on."

Some of the hardest tension to deal with is the stress we don't understand. Each of us needs to know the cause for the friction. Otherwise we are left to guess and often we guess wrong.

Jesus Christ handled it in a cool way when there was tension among his disciples. He knew they were arguing but he didn't know why. The Son of God didn't worry about it. He didn't stew. He didn't internalize it and blame himself. His approach was clean and direct. Jesus asked them what they were arguing about.

Don't stay bewildered. Some parents may not give an answer but they need to be asked. Give them a chance to explain. Be straightforward and tell them you want to know.

"What are you arguing with them about?" he asked.

Mark 9:16

Keep thinking

1. Is there a problem you need to bring up to a parent?
2. When would be a good time to ask the question you need to ask?

Speak Up!

Do you have conversations floating around in your brain? Are there a lot of things you want to say that you've never said? Most of us are that way.

When Christopher's dad left to marry someone else, Christopher wanted to ask a few questions. He even wanted to complain. But instead he said almost nothing at all.

Today Christopher repeats his questions and complaints over and over to himself. Unfortunately he has never said them out loud.

With Sarah it is different. Her mother means the world to her. She is so proud of what her mom does, how she talks, and even how she looks. Sarah would like to tell her mother how important she is.

This teen knows what she wants to say, she simply can't get the words out.

Every day in school Angela sits quietly and never volunteers. She knows most of the answers, but still she is afraid of embarrassing herself. History, math, English each pass by and Angela merely holds her tongue.

But the correct answers run around inside her brain. And almost every day she wishes she could let them out.

Some teens don't seem to have any trouble expressing themselves. To listen to them, you would believe they say everything they think. Maybe we don't want to be that open, but many of us wish we could open up more and let it out.

Most quiet people need some relief. They need to take some chances and let more sentences roll. There are too many conversations floating inside. Their brains start forming log jams with so many words backed up.

If you aren't used to saying how you feel, it will take some courage to begin. It will take special effort to force yourself to speak up. But after you do it a few times, it will become easier to express yourself.

Many people who talk a great deal are people who had to make themselves do it. They decided it wasn't good to stay lost in a silent world.

There are opinions you need to express.

There is happiness that needs to get out.

There are fears you need to voice.

There are disappointments that must be said.

There are dreams you want to tell.

Don't clog up your mind with too many unspoken feelings.

"I must speak and find relief; I must open my lips and reply."

Job 32:20

Keep thinking

1. Is there something you very much want to tell someone?
2. Why not say it today?

Breaking Up

Jessica couldn't imagine any fifteen-year-old happier than she was. For the past six months she and Toby enjoyed going together. They walked the mall, went to movies, and even bowled sometimes. In three more months Toby would get his driver's license and would probably be able to borrow his father's car.

Once in a while they argued, but nothing big. They were always able to make up, and making up was half the fun.

For a high school sophomore, life couldn't have been much better. Then this note blew her away.

> "Dear Jessica,
> It's hard to explain but I've found someone else. See ya around.
>
> Toby"

Talk about an arrow through the heart! Talk about the world caving in! Jessica was crushed to dust.

What would she do now? she wondered. What would she say? "Oh, no, Toby and I don't go together anymore. He dropped me like a spider."

There was something she wanted. It wasn't so much Toby himself as it was the relationship. There were good times together, places to go, a lot of laughs. The relationship was dependable. It was hard to lose the connection. Now her heart was broken. Jessica was lonely, embarrassed, and stressed out.

Breaking up is a big stressor. We feel shocked and rocked. We wonder how we will struggle on and meet the demands of each day.

When it happens, it's all right to feel lousy. That's normal. People don't usually take loss easily, and losing the person you were going with is one of the most painful.

If it happens, we need to tell someone how we feel. Get it out. Say it like it is. We have trouble getting over a loss if we hold that loss inside.

Someone we especially want to tell is God. God cares about all kinds of loss, whether it's flunking a class, losing a jacket, or breaking up with someone special.

Not only is God a great listener, but he also can bring other good things into our lives. God always has time to help heal a broken heart.

"He heals the brokenhearted and binds up their wounds."

Psalm 147:3

Keep thinking

1. Has anyone ever broken your heart?
2. How did you handle it?
3. Did you take time to share it with God?

Will the Balloon Pop?

Do you ever feel pressure in your chest building up like a hot air balloon? It's as if you are taking air in but you aren't letting enough air out. How much air can a set of lungs hold anyway? Balloons pop if they have too much air, and you might wonder if there is some way you might blow up, too.

Many of us feel this way before a play begins or a date or a test or some other big event. There is uncertainty about the occasion and a need to do well. Are we going to be good enough and do well when it really counts?

We all go through this big build-up. Sometimes we think it happens almost daily.

Fortunately there is a way to let the air out of the balloon. This brings relief immediately and everyone can do it.

There are two parts to this exercise and it only takes a minute or so.

First, breathe in and out slowly. Take deep breaths. Think about letting the air out of your balloon. The balloon has gotten too tight and needs to be deflated. Take three, four, five deep breaths.

Second, as you inhale and exhale, repeat this simple Bible verse:

"This is the day the Lord has made; let us rejoice and be glad in it."

Psalm 118:24

Deep breathing will probably help by itself, but coupled with the verse the exercise is even more effective.

The verse helps us put the events of the day into a spiritual context. God gave us this day, so we have plenty of reason to be happy about it. The most important thing about today isn't the test we are going to take. More importantly, God will be with us no matter how we do on the exam.

There are physical exercises we can do to make the day go better. There are also spiritual exercises reminding us that God gave us this day and we can be glad he did.

Breathe in. Breathe out.

"This is the day the Lord has made; let us rejoice and be glad in it."

Psalm 118:24

Keep thinking

1. Have you tried the "hot air balloon" exercise? How did it work?
2. Are you able to accept this day as a gift from God?

Pulled Apart

Every day Wade had to make important choices. In one corner of the school they were planning parties. Down the hall they were passing around cigarettes that smelled funny. Upstairs, in the school library, they were selling answers to the physics exam. Next to the furnace room someone was showing off a new knife he bought cheap.

Some days were calm but no day was easy. There were always decisions for Wade to make. Was he going to move with this group or was he going to try and wade into that circle?

Decision making is normally hard, and for teens it may be especially difficult. There are so many things you face for the first time. You don't have as much experience making choices on your own. And if you mess up, you could meet serious consequences for years to come.

When a teen, like Wade, happens to be a Christian he has to wrestle with his special convictions. As a follower of Christ, should he reject the choices that could mess him up?

Wade said that on the one hand:

Being a Christian made it easier because it gave him a set of values.

But on the other hand:

Being a Christian gave him conflicts because it made him feel bad about cheating and drugging and lying.

Christians often feel pulled apart. Sometimes that hurts. But the good news is that Christians can handle each day with a set of values. Those values tell us we can't lie or steal or be unfaithful or hurt our bodies or a great deal more.

If we follow Jesus Christ, there are times when we will be able to stand firm though many choices try to pull us apart. We can resist pressure better because we accept God's values.

A man in the Bible named Jethro told his son-in-law, Moses, that there was a way to fight the pressure. He said:

> "If you follow [my] advice, and if the Lord agrees, you will be able to endure the pressures, and there will be peace and harmony in the camp."
>
> Exodus 18:23 (TLB)

Keep thinking

1. How do you make the moral choices you face at school?
2. Do you apply your Christian values to the difficult situations?

To Cheat or Not . . .

"I don't usually ask you for anything," Breanna droned. "But we were away most of the weekend and then Todd came over last night."

"It just doesn't seem right," Karla fidgeted. "Besides Mr. Muske will know if our answers are exactly alike."

"He'll never know," Breanna pleaded. "I'll reword a few of the answers so they'll be different. Come on, Karla, you gotta."

"I spent hours working on these questions." Karla opened her book looking for her folded paper. "Then our computer started acting up. It was late before I got done." She handed her homework to her friend.

"Thanks. You've saved my life. I've got study hall first period. I'll copy it then and give this back to you in class." Breanna gathered her books and hurried away.

"After all," Karla mumbled to herself. "What are friends for?"

Scenes like that happen almost every day in most schools. Struggling students are not the only ones who copy homework or cheat on tests. Some surveys tell us that most students who get A's and B's cheat on schoolwork sometime. Sadly some of them cheat often.

The practice of cheating is so widespread that many students don't think it is wrong. They believe it's all right as long as they don't get caught.

It's never easy to resist temptation. Someone else's school paper or answers to the quiz are usually available for the asking. A person has to show genuine strength to turn down a quick solution to his problems.

Like all temptations, cheating can be resisted. It may take planning. It may take willpower. It may take discipline. But some young people and adults reject the opportunity to cheat. It can be done.

The Bible tells us this: There is no temptation that we can't resist. We all meet temptation regularly. And God promises us that none will come our way that we can't reject.

"But I have to cheat if I am going to get by" is a false statement. Cheating is a powerful pressure but it can be resisted.

> *"Every test that you have experienced is the kind that normally comes to people. But God keeps his promise, and he will not allow you to be tested beyond your power to remain firm; at the time you are put to the test, he will give you the strength to endure it, and so provide you with a way out."*
> *1 Corinthians 10:13 (TEV)*

Keep thinking

1. Do you feel pressure to cheat?
2. Do you shake it off and refuse to cheat?

The Vodka Revolt

In 1991 a dozen men tried to overthrow the Russian government. Television and the newspapers were filled with the story. The coup soon failed and the government stayed intact.

Many people feel that the flow of alcohol was the basic reason for the revolt. No doubt the twelve people had grievances against the government leadership, but would they have acted if they hadn't been bending their elbows too much?

Reportedly, several of the men downed two or three glasses of vodka as they discussed their plans. Vodka has long been a favorite alcoholic drink among Russians. It is a colorless liquor often made from rye or wheat. In such a cold climate Russians are known to have serious alcohol problems, as in many other countries.

The revolution failed; some of the plotters were drunk when they were arrested.

How many discussions turn into dumb situations simply because alcohol got out of hand? Car crashes, family fights, shouting matches, murders, robberies too often find their origin in a bottle.

Every person should be reminded of the terrible damage that alcohol can do.

"Wine is a mocker, strong drink a brawler;
and whoever is led astray by it is not wise."
                                   Proverbs 20:1 (RSV)

Keep thinking

1. Have you seen trouble caused by alcohol?
2. What is your attitude toward alcohol?

Dress Stress

When you pick out the latest top and pair of jeans at the local store, does your parent react by saying, "Forget it"? If so, you are probably suffering from "dress stress." You want clothes that match your taste and your culture and this sends Mom or Dad into fashion shock.

Don't think you're abnormal. Parents and teens often lock horns over styles, prices, colors and materials. Frankly, this wastes a great deal of energy and creates far too much turmoil.

It isn't unusual for teens to go to extremes in their clothing and looks. One month hairstyles are short and the next they are long. Wait another month and everyone has messages clipped on the backs of their skulls. Clothes get big, then the colors become loud. In a few months they might be back to worn jeans with torn knees.

Teen dress is a world that most adults don't understand. It's hard for teens to explain that world because young people can't always spell it out either. But teen feelings are real.

To be fair, don't expect parents to simply understand. When a teen wants to reduce his "dress stress," he has to be willing to patiently discuss clothing with the significant adults in his life.

Some ways to do that are:

Take a parent to your favorite clothing store to look around.

Bring friends over who wear the kind of clothes you want.

Be willing and patient to answer your parent's questions about gang clothing or whatever.

Ask your parent what he or she wore as a teen and why. (You won't believe it.)

Keep your behavior reasonably sane so you won't appear to have lost your senses.

Be tolerant of your parent's failure to see the need.

Be willing to compromise. No one gets everything he wants.

Keep your sense of humor and keep hoping. Teens who don't lose their cool and are careful to explain things often are able to change their parents.

Write this verse down and place it on your mirror. Write it on a book cover and carry it to school. Stick it under a magnet on the fridge.

"Be joyful in hope."

Romans 12:12

Keep thinking

1. How understanding has your parent been about clothing?
2. How can you explain your situation a little more clearly to your parent?

These Are the Facts

Young people don't want to be preached at about AIDS. Especially they don't like older people telling them what to do. They may listen to people their age, but they are suspicious of adults.

All right. No sermon. No plea. No condemnation. Instead I will list a few of the simple facts as of this writing.

1. Half of the people in the world who get the AIDS virus are between the ages of 15 and 24.
2. The virus (HIV) is moving rapidly and silently through the youth community.
3. There is no cure for the disease.
4. Teenage girls contract the disease more rapidly than teenage boys.
5. The virus turns into full-blown AIDS more frequently in boys than in girls.
6. Did I mention that there is no cure for this disease?

The Bible emphasizes "speaking the truth in love" (Ephesians 4:15.) This is the truth.

Getting Dissed

"Dissed" is a word that entered our vocabulary a few years ago. It means that a person has been treated with disrespect.

If someone promises to meet us at the movie but doesn't show, we feel ticked. When they don't show and don't even bother to call and explain why, we feel like they don't have much respect for us. We've been dissed.

No one likes it. Most of us can still remember a time when another person showed no regard for how we felt.

When Jason's father promised to go shopping with him for a new coat, the fifteen-year-old got his hopes up. He didn't see his father much and wanted to get together with him.

An hour before they were to meet, Jason got a phone call. Some of his dad's friends were going golfing and his dad really wanted to go. He knew Jason would understand, he said; besides they could go shopping next week. Jason was dissed.

It happens to everyone. But that doesn't make it good and it doesn't make it right. Being treated with disrespect makes us feel like a fly that has just been swatted at.

All of our lives we hear about treating adults with respect. We're told to give respect to the elderly, to teachers, to police, to neighbors. But it's important to offer respect to everyone.

Teens deserve respect.
Children deserve respect.
Homeless deserve respect.
Mentally ill deserve respect.
Strangers deserve respect.
Minorities deserve respect.

When we don't get respect, we feel hurt and get uptight. Sometimes we are tempted to hurt others because we are ignored or mistreated. But that's always wrong.

Marriages fail because couples don't respect each other. Parent/teen relationships suffer when they fail to show mutual respect. Neighbors fight because they lack respect.

A man blared his stereo so loud that it disturbed the person next door. The man said that was too bad, he had a right to play his music. Maybe that was so, but he showed no respect for his neighbor.

The Bible teaches us a better way. It tells us to respect everyone. All of us are important. All of us are made in the image of God. The young, the old, and everyone in between should be handled with consideration.

> *"Show respect for everyone."*
> 1 Peter 2:17 (TLB)

Keep thinking

1. Is there someone you have been showing little respect for lately?
2. Can you ask God to help you change your attitude?

Staying Young

Don't be in a hurry to grow up. There is plenty of time for that later. Growing up too fast will cause you to miss the enjoyment of youth.

The Hotlines and Helplines that offer telephone help for teens tell us two things are changing:

1. The subjects teens want to talk about are more serious and deadly than they used to be.
2. The youth who call are younger.

Years ago high school seniors used to worry over the effects of alcohol or drugs or sexual diseases or suicide. Today it is seventh graders and younger who call to ask the same questions.

Early teens are torn. One day adults tell them to grow up and act their age. The next day adults tell them they are just kids and don't know anything.

There's a hurry to grow up. Teens want to:

try things	get experience
be adventurous	act older
be free	rebel
experiment	get wheels
try alcohol	check out drugs

It's like they are on a roller coaster and they want to see how fast they can go downhill.

Most of us don't like to be told to slow down. "Take your time" sounds like a real dud. Teens think grandmothers and heart patients should slow down.

The mad race to act older can tear teens apart. They feel the need to hurry up and get to the next stage of life. The hurrying tears them up and leaves them exhausted.

A big part of the problem is too many people trying too many things before they're ready. It takes a cool head for someone to say, "No thanks; I'll wait."

The Bible tells us to enjoy our youth while we have it. Young people can appreciate life one day at a time. There's no need to get involved in fast drugs, fast sex, fast cars, and fast money. Don't feel bad simply because you decided to make the most out of staying young.

> "Be happy, young man, while you are young, and let your heart give you joy in the days of your youth. Follow the ways of your heart and whatever your eyes see, but know that for all these things God will bring you to judgment."
>
> Ecclesiastes 11:9

Keep thinking

1. Is there anything you think you are trying too soon?
2. What do you enjoy about being your age right now?

Hated in L.A.

This is what the F.B.I. told the people in church: There is a plot to spray your church with machine gun fire and to blow it up. Your enemies are racists who hope to create chaos and start a "holy war."

Try to imagine the Sunday morning announcements at your church when the minister explains how the church was almost attacked and its people killed. Shock would ripple across the congregation. Who can say how we would feel or what we would do?

In this case the 2,000 members of the First African Methodist Episcopal Church in Los Angeles decided they would wage a peaceful war on those who hated them. The pastor told the congregation they were a love group. They would not become a hate group.

The natural reaction is to hate those who hate us. Unfortunately, hate is a great deal of work. If we hate others, we use a lot of energy. If we hate others, our hate changes us to become someone we didn't want to become. When we hate the hater, the hater wins.

Hate is hard to deal with. We become blinded when we take the hate route. It's harder to see goodness or love or kindness or happiness because hate places blinders over our eyes.

Christians are asked to act like peculiar people. We are told to love our enemies (Matthew 5:43, 44). That's what the pastor of the church in Los Angeles told the congregation. The ability to love those who hate us can be a gift from God. Anyone can love their friends.

All of us have burdens to carry around. Maybe we have trouble with a friend. We don't have enough money. We can't get a date and our CD player is slowly dying. None of us needs the extra load of hating someone. It's a bummer all the way around.

> *"But the one who hates his brother is in the darkness and walks in the darkness, and does not know where he is going because the darkness has blinded his eyes."*
>
> *1 John 2:11 (NAS)*

Keep thinking

1. Is there someone you used to hate but now enjoy being around? How did that happen?
2. Is there someone you want to stop hating? Have you talked to God about it?

Driving Like a Madman

A young couple in Nebraska spent a Saturday afternoon arguing. Finally the wife could stand it no more, grabbed the keys to the car, and raced away down the road. A few minutes later her husband decided to jump in the pickup and go after her.

On a back road he discovered her tire tracks and followed them. Near a river, he saw skid marks leading into the water. Staring into the dark water he could see the wheels of a vehicle.

Instantly he dove into the water to rescue his wife. The door on her side wouldn't open, but he finally forced the passenger door ajar. Freeing his wife, he held her out of the water to try to get her breathing again. Once on shore he performed CPR and she revived.

Afterward the couple said they had learned a great deal from the incident. When you're mad, they warned, don't think you are a race car driver. There isn't anything worth getting that mad about, they added.

It's hard to imagine how many drivers are on the roads with grouchy attitudes. Some are depressed and don't care where they're driving. Some are under tremendous stress and are thinking about other things. A few are so angry they wouldn't be afraid of hurting another driver.

Smart people take time to get control of themselves before they start the engine. One sudden thoughtless decision could result in a tragic accident.

When you sit down behind the wheel, say to yourself, "Calm down. I have to be ready to drive now."

The Bible tells about King Jehu, who loved to race off in his chariot. One day a lookout saw a chariot tearing across the countryside and he knew who it looked like.

He said, "The driving is like that of Jehu son of Nimshi—he drives like a madman" (2 Kings 9:20).

Take some deep breaths. Wait a few minutes. Think about the vehicle, the road, and the people on it. Don't let stress make you drive like a nut.

Keep thinking

1. Have you ever done something foolish while you were in a rage?
2. What do you do to calm yourself?

Touchy Touchy

When I entered junior high school, the transition from grade school was very hard. Students came from various parts of the city, forcing us to mix with people we didn't grow up with. New faces, new clothes, new styles, new ways of talking, even new leaders in the groups. The upheaval and turmoil of so much change was scary.

I can remember being both excited and frightened on my first day at the new school. Mostly I was frightened. How was I, a new kid, going to fare among all of these noisy, energetic, fast-moving teenagers?

Unfortunately I decided to put on a firm face and defend myself. I didn't want anyone pushing me around, so I decided to act tough. If anyone messed with me I would take them on and fight it out.

With that attitude I had no trouble finding people to fight. If someone said the wrong thing to me, I pushed them immediately. I remember one poor guy didn't talk to me in the hall, so I dared him to come outside and fight. He showed up and we had a messy battle.

Not that I was very good at fighting. Sometimes I took an awful beating. But I believed combat was the best way to communicate and to protect myself.

It's fair to say I was touchy. If anyone said the wrong thing to me or ignored me, I was all over them like grass on a lawn.

Fortunately two things happened to rescue me. One, I graduated into high school where the atmosphere was calmer. And two, I became a Christian. Becoming a Christian didn't change everything about me, but it made many things better. Now I had a sense of acceptance, of forgiveness, and even of purpose. I also had a new set of friends at the youth group in my neighborhood church.

I became less touchy. Words or names or insults or being left out no longer sent me into a rage. The introduction of Christ into my life made me less fearful and less of a hothead.

If I'm not careful I can still get provoked easily, but it's not like it used to be. Growing up has made a difference and finding peace in Jesus Christ has had a big effect.

> *"Do not be quickly provoked in your spirit,*
> *for anger resides in the lap of fools."*
> *Ecclesiastes 7:9*

Keep thinking

1. Sometimes are you touchy?
2. Why are you touchy?
3. Does being a Christian help reduce your touchiness?

Violent Reaction

Do you ever get so angry that you lash out and break something? Have you ever lost your temper and hit someone? Many of us use violence to express our frustrations and anger.

A nineteen-year-old was upset because someone took her stereo set. Convinced that another teen knew where the set was, the nineteen-year-old killed the other teen. She is scheduled to spend the rest of her life in prison.

A young man failed his chemistry test. Distraught over this setback he took a shotgun to school. Marching directly to the chemistry class he shot and seriously wounded the teacher.

Unable to face his parents when he broke curfew, a teen in the Midwest loaded his rifle and murdered his father.

Each of these young people became frustrated and didn't know how to cope with anger. Unable or unwilling to talk about their problems, they expressed themselves violently. It looks like members of our society are turning more and more to force as a way of dealing with pressure.

There is a man in the Old Testament who experienced a lot of major pain. His house burned down, his children died, his health failed, and even his friends started to dump on him. It would have been easy for Job to go into a rage and start knocking heads around. Fortunately Job looked for more constructive ways to deal with his frustration and loss.

One of the ways the ancient Israelite chose was prayer and not violence. Instead of grabbing a spear or a lance or a club, Job decided to discuss it with God. God is a good listener. God is patient. God is understanding. God is also able to change the way we think if we spend time talking to him.

Can you picture Job early one morning making a hard decision? He looks at his lance propped up against the wall and he's tempted to grab it. Maybe he should show his miserable friends a thing or two. But he pauses. He thinks it over. Then Job gets a grip and sits down. Job has decided to look for wisdom by talking to God.

Sometimes we have to decide to do the sane thing instead of the violent thing.

"My face is red with weeping, deep shadows ring my eyes; yet my hands have been free of violence and my prayer is pure."
Job 16:16–17

Keep thinking

1. How do you handle your anger when you feel like hitting or breaking?
2. Have you ever tried to calm down by talking to God for a minute or two? Could you try it next time?

What Are Green Teens?

Green Teens aren't Martians or creatures who live at the bottom of some riverbed in Iceland. Green Teens are young people who became tired of griping about how bad things are and decided to do something about it.

These youth have stopped listening and have begun to act.

One excellent example can be found at North Cobb High School in Atlanta, Georgia. For a long time the students heard how the environment has been abused, stripped, stomped, and pickled. They saw polluted rivers, dead ducks, and decaying trees.

Since griping leads to frustration and frustration leads to fingernail chewing, it is harmful to gripe forever. The best thing to do is get active, and that's what these Green Teens did. They joined a group that is trying to restore Mount Mitchell.

Acid rains had wrecked the trees and soil around the mountain. Minerals had been washed out of the ground and the mountain was in sad condition.

Green Teens jumped in and looked for a solution. This led them, under professional supervision, to start spreading certain minerals on the mountain. Today the soil is becoming rich again and trees are being planted in the once depleted earth.

All of us hear how bad things are. If we hear bad news all the time we become edgy, unhappy, and even grouchy. But if we hear the truth and do something about it, we start to feel healthy, productive, and glad.

Anyone can recite what's wrong with the world. It takes a special person to do something.

It would be interesting to ask a group to raise their hands if they have ever heard of:

homelessness	poverty
hunger	racism
wars	illiteracy
acid rain	orphans
crime	

Most hands would be raised. It might be another matter to ask the same group how many have done something to remedy the problems.

Listening to reports, complaints, information, and stories can build up our dissatisfaction. On the other hand if we do something, we can feel great relief.

"Do not merely listen to the word, and so deceive yourselves. Do what it says."
James 1:22

Keep thinking

1. What really bugs you about this world?
2. What are you going to do to help?

Feeling Dumpy

Recently I asked a group of teens what they do when they feel down and depressed. How do they get a grip and survive the pits? These are some of the solutions they use to come back to life:

They sleep. It's easy for young people to get worn out. Often they think they have limitless energy and get involved in too many things.

They eat. Many teens eat irregularly or simply eat junk. Others are on diets. Frequently a crisis can be handled better if we first eat sensibly.

They drive (long and fast). This is what they said. Naturally this is dangerous because the driver has trouble concentrating, and accidents are far more likely if the driver is downcast.

They talk. Most talk to people their age but some talk to adults. Others talk to God because God is a good listener and God can change things.

They mope. Not always the most helpful, but a few minutes of creative moping is understandable. If you choose to mope, set a time limit. This can be controlled.

They divert. They put their minds on something else. You have strong brain power with which you usually can change your concentration.

They reason with themselves. They give themselves positive talk. "This period of depression will most likely pass. The sun will shine tomorrow."

Other ways to fight the dumpy feelings are to go to a movie or rent one, get active (bowl, skate, etc.), invite a friend over, make something, bake something, read something.

There are alternatives to feeling dumpy. Sometimes friends come over and rescue us even when they didn't know we were depressed. (I always look at them as doing the work of God.)

God is very concerned about our bad days. He isn't interested in chewing us out for being down. Rather, God is eager to help us as we also help ourselves.

> *"Why are you downcast, O my soul? Why so disturbed within me?*
> *Put your hope in God, for I will yet praise him, my Savior and my God."*
>
> *Psalm 42:5*

Keep thinking

1. How do you deal with feeling dumpy?
2. Is there another way of coping you would like to try?

Teen Abuse

We hear a great deal about child abuse but not nearly so much about adolescent abuse. Each year hundreds of thousands of teens are seriously mistreated and abused. The problem is that many young people never report it. They live under conditions where they are hurt, neglected, or sexually used, but they don't say anything.

Many teens kid about being abused. They talk about low allowances and strict curfews, but they know this isn't really dangerous. The real problem is that many young people are being injured physically, sexually, and mentally. Those teens need help.

The teen who is abused needs to tell a friend, a doctor, a teacher, a counselor, a minister, or a parent, or call an abuse line. The number should be in your phone book, probably inside the front or back cover.

Often teens are reluctant to speak up. They are afraid they won't be taken seriously. They are embarrassed that something terrible has happened to them. There are people and agencies who will not only take them seriously but who are able to help.

It would be foolish to suffer silently. Too many teens are seriously hurt. A few are killed.

Maybe you know someone who is being abused by a friend, a neighbor, a relative, a stranger, a parent, or on a date. When you see bruises or they cry a great deal or they tell you about sexual acts they have to endure, let them know that they can find help. Also tell them it's smart to reach out to a dependable authority figure when they are in physical or emotional pain.

We aren't being nosy or gossipy if we make a suggestion to someone we know. If he says, "Oh, it's nothing; I just fell down the stairs," he may be telling the truth. Let it go. But what if he shows up later with another bad bruise? Then we might want to say something again. "If there's a problem, you know you can get help" might be a good sentence.

Most of us aren't able to force people to get help. If they won't get help, it isn't our fault. Teens aren't expected to "rescue" other teens. But it does make sense to say something to a friend who appears to be under terrible pressure.

If we need help, it would be smart to go for it. When our friend needs help, the caring thing to do is to ask a question or make a suggestion.

God tells us to call out if we have a problem. Sometimes we need to call out to people as well as to God for help.

"In my day of trouble I will call to you, for you will answer me."

Psalm 86:7

Keep thinking

1. Is there a friend you are worried about?
2. Do you need to remind him or her that help can be found?
3. Is this a good day to bring that up?

The Problem Shift

Concern has a good side. We should be concerned about hunger and war and diseases and people without hope. We also should be concerned about ourselves. All of us should do our jobs well, study, have our health checked, keep close contact with God, eat right, and get a reasonable amount of exercise.

Sometimes problems arise because we spend too much time concerned about *numero uno*.

Imagine you find a pimple on your hand. The first thing you are likely to do is pick it open. Throughout the day you will probably push and squeeze it. The wound will try to heal itself and develop a scab, but it cannot if you keep bothering it. And bother it you will. Pull, scrape, poke. Eventually the sore will need disinfectant and a bandage.

The pimple would have benefitted from a little neglect.

Some problems are aggravated by too much attention. Not every trouble should be pampered, analyzed, and solved. A few should be ignored and allowed to heal themselves.

One of the best ways to divert our attention from our own dilemmas is to help others with their problems. It's called the problem shift.

At least once a week we need to help other people with their problems. We need to take the spotlight off our difficulties and shift the light onto another person.

We might want to help a friend, a relative, an elderly person, or even a stranger at school. Maybe a blind person would like to be read to. Maybe a shut-in would appreciate a visit. Why not volunteer to baby-sit once a week for a neighbor family or even for your own parents?

Some teens teach classes, work soup kitchens, deliver meals, or work in hospitals. For a few hours a week they become involved in the needs of others.

It seems like the happiest people are those who find purpose by serving others. The unhappiest may be those who become self-centered and overwhelmed by their own pain.

God encourages us to climb out of our shells and look for people who need us.

> *"And look out for one another's interests, not just for your own."*
>
> *Philippians 2:4 (TEV)*

Keep thinking

1. Are you presently helping someone else? If so, how?
2. Who can you think of that could use your help?

Christian Meditation

Does meditation sound spooky? Do we picture someone sitting for hours, staring into space, legs folded, possibly chanting phrases over and over? Maybe we have even thought of meditation as someone on drugs looking at tiny dots, trying to expand consciousness.

Christian meditation doesn't mean any of that. Christian meditation means we take time out to think about God and his Son, Jesus Christ. We think about who they are and what they do and how they interact with people.

Meditation has tremendous benefits:

Good for our health: Calms us down and might lower our blood pressure.

Good for our minds: Allows us to get outside our daily problems.

Good for our soul: Causes us to contemplate the goodness of God and all of his gifts and activities.

One minute, ten minutes, or thirty minutes a day gives us the chance to get in contact with reality. The existence of God and God's work among people is reality.

Christian meditation can be done almost any place. Standing on a bus, sitting in a tree, in the back row at study hall, in your room, or in the back booth at the local pizza place. It's discouraged while driving motorcycles, piloting jet planes, or playing basketball.

Some of the things we might think about while meditating are:

God's unconditional love
God's laws for the universe
God's creative works
God's promises to us
God's hope for tomorrow
God's desire for peace

The subjects for meditation are almost limitless. If we use the Bible and read a verse or more, it could prove a help to our spiritual thoughts.

Meditating could be done on and off all day long. For most of us a set time and a regular place would be helpful. The practice is much like a spiritual time-out. In a nutty life with deadlines, goals, and constant demands, it's the kind of relief we could use.

"We meditate upon your kindness and your love."

Psalm 48:9 (TLB)

Keep thinking

1. When might you get in a few minutes of meditation?
2. What do you hope Christian meditation will accomplish in your life?

Switching Friends

Many people switch friends so they can climb the social ladder. They want to be accepted into a club or get invited to better parties or look cool around school. We've all seen that happen and we have our own opinions of those kinds of moves.

With Christine it was a different story. She had become close friends with several girls who were living on the edge. They were smoking and drinking and running with a high-risk group of guys. The girls seemed to like lying and cheating. Even if they didn't need to lie, they would do it anyway.

This circle of friends was accepting and caring. If Christine wasn't around for a day or two the girls would call or drop by. They missed the fourteen-year-old and seemed to like her.

After six months of hanging out with the crowd, Christine realized she had some serious decisions to make. Every week she became more like them and less like herself. It was like an octopus changing its color to match the rocks around it. This teen was losing her identity in order to blend in with the crowd.

Unfortunately, it was the wrong crowd.

When another friend from church invited Christine to go bowling, she recognized it was an important decision. Her old friends would laugh if she went. They would probably try to pull her away and keep her. The old group cared that much.

Switching friends is one of the hardest things any of us can do. Friends offer security, some self-worth, a form of love, a social outlet, and sometimes even protection. It takes a really strong person to recognize when a friend is hurting him. It takes an even stronger person to switch friends when he needs to.

It's a hard step, and the earlier someone makes the move the better. The minute we realize that a friendship is taking us in a direction we shouldn't go, that's the best time to find other friends. Some teens would give anything to be able to throw off the old crowd, but their attachments are so deep they no longer know how to cut the ropes that tie them.

The Bible tells us to take a hike. Move on, move out, move up, move away, but move. Don't wait until the ropes get too tight. Sit at another table. Join a club. Find a youth group. If necessary sign up for bird watching and listen for yellow finches on Saturday mornings.

If we know a bad deal is coming together, we need to put on traveling shoes—now.

> "Therefore come out from them and be separate, says the Lord."
>
> *2 Corinthians 6:17*

Keep thinking

1. Are you involved with friends where you shouldn't be?
2. How can you separate from those friends?

Help the Kids!

Most children have great respect for teenagers. They see teens as cool people who wear neat clothes, go to interesting places, and have a great amount of freedom. Often they think middle school and high school are the top of the world and they would love to be there.

Many elementary-age kids live in dangerous communities. At only ten years of age, some are making serious, life-altering decisions. Too many become attached to gangs or get involved in drugs or even run away from home. Children often don't have much chance if they get swallowed up by the wrong crowd.

A police sergeant on a big city anti-gang unit recently said that the risk faced by preteens keeps growing. The pressure they face is often too much for young lives to handle.

When I was a preteen I greatly admired the teens who were in high school. They looked like they had it together and I wanted to grow up to be like them.

This is why teenagers in churches can provide good role models for children. They could organize game nights, sports events, craft workshops, car modeling classes, computer sessions, and other events geared for kids. Teens might choose to use adult supervisors.

Teenagers have a large capacity to care for others. Many are not the self-centered, self-seeking youth that adults make them out to be. With a little encouragement teens might respond to a call to help children.

If a couple of teens were to go to an adult at their church with a desire to help kids, the ball could start rolling. Before long more teens could get involved and a handful of children could receive the attention they need exactly when it is so valuable.

As followers of Christ we are called to serve others. Teenagers are not too young to serve and children certainly need the help. Look around and see if there are kids who could use a few good role models so they won't go astray.

> *"And ourselves as your servants for Jesus' sake."*
>
> *2 Corinthians 4:5 (TEV)*

Keep thinking

1. What kid do you know who could use a little guidance and activity?
2. What adult do you know who might help get a project going?

Walk Away!

The newspaper said it hadn't been easy for Brian. Formerly he had belonged to a gang in Chicago, but he didn't want it anymore. Brian stopped wearing gang clothes, refused to hang out with them, and, of course, rejected the violence.

Despite his best intentions, he still had trouble avoiding conflicts. If he met someone from another gang or even a member of his old gang, the temptation was strong to get into an argument or trade menacing looks.

Brian's friends and relatives always told him to just walk away from trouble. The advice sounded simple, but it wasn't easy for this teen. More than once harsh words were spoken at old hangouts and blows were almost traded.

One Monday evening Brian accidentally ran into three gang members at a food store. They stared at him down the aisle. Brian's brother told him to just walk away. But Brian felt he couldn't.

Harsh words were said. A couple of fists were swung. Then the noise rang out. It was a loud, short, crisp sound. One of the gang members had fired a shot. A single bullet slammed into Brian's forehead. He dropped immediately and his brother dropped to his knees to hold him. As the gang members fled, Brian's life ran out on the tile floor.

No one wants to be a coward. It's hard for most of us to be insulted and simply walk away. But often the really brave people and the smartest teens are the ones who have the sense to leave.

When we see another person acting dumb or talking crazy, it may be time to relocate. As the tension rises, the risk is great that something stupid could happen.

Other people are acting like fools if they try to start trouble. If we get sucked into the argument, we act like fools, too.

"Walk away" may sound too simple. But the coolest young people manage to pull it off. Often it takes courage to leave a bad scene.

The Bible puts it this way:

> *"Run from anything that gives you the evil thoughts that young men often have, but stay close to anything that makes you want to do right."*
>
> 2 Timothy 2:22 (TLB)

Keep thinking

1. Can you think of a time when you walked away from a bad situation?
2. Can you remember when you wish you had walked away?
3. Is there a bad deal that you need to walk away from now?

Empty Clouds

All Matt wanted was some relief. Every day he had to make decisions.

Was he ready for the government test?
Should he skip track practice?
Did his shirt look good enough?
Should he get a date?
What about the part-time job?
Would his mom catch him lying?

These were the kinds of choices he had to make on a regular basis.

In order to cope with all he had to do, Matt started to look for relief. Everyone has to find ways to cope in life, and this teenager was looking for a way.

For a while Matt tried cigarettes. He wondered if they would help soothe his nerves enough to relax. When that didn't work, he went to smokeless tobacco. That didn't calm him and he soon found himself craving for more.

Alcohol was a natural choice. It was easy to get and most of his friends drank. Beer made him high so he could forget for a while, but soon he crashed back into reality. Often Matt was far worse off the next day than before he drank.

Marijuana was next. It gave him a buzz and made him feel cool. But grass never did solve one of his problems. When the buzz became less, he wondered if a more serious drug might be the ticket.

Matt went through each substance. He had high hopes for some relief. Sometimes they did help him forget for a few hours, but none gave him the ability to sift it all out.

Drugs and substances were all empty clouds. Each looked like it held the promise of relief, but they all passed by without delivering the goods. Instead, they made Matt's problems bigger and bigger.

The Bible tells us about people who look like the real thing but are only phonies. They say the right words but they aren't the genuine article.

Alcohol and drugs might look like the way to deal with stress. The fact is they don't solve anything. Generally they make the pressure worse. We all need to remember that sometimes.

"They are clouds without rain, blown along by the wind; autumn trees, without fruit and uprooted—twice dead."

Jude 12

Keep thinking

1. Have you tried some dumb ways to escape pressure? Name one.
2. Name one good way you have learned to deal with stress.

Stop It!

How many of us create pressure in our lives? We can't blame all of our problems on outside forces. Often we produce stress by causing conflicts within ourselves.

Michelle worked at a local convenience store on Tuesday and Friday evenings. She didn't make much money, but each week she managed to steal three or four dollars. Because she was stealing, Michelle was constantly afraid she would get caught.

No one else was causing her tension. Michelle's own behavior left her full of distress.

With Ryan the problem was lying. He told his parents that he studied at Jeremy's house on Wednesday nights. His parents knew his friend was a whiz at computers and that Ryan needed all the help he could get.

In reality Ryan played video games at the mall on Wednesday nights. Each week he worried that his parents would find out and get very angry. He also knew that his report card would soon call the entire scheme into question.

Drinking alcohol was a passion for Sarah. On Saturdays the high school junior would go to a friend's house and often they had beer brought in. Late at night Sarah would go home with great fear. What if her mother caught her? There would be a

71

terrible price to pay. She would probably be grounded and lose a lot of privileges.

In spite of the possible consequences Sarah was willing to take the risk. What she wanted to do was more important than the anxiety it gave her.

Teens frequently complain about the pressures that are placed on them. Sometimes that's true. But just as often they themselves weave a spider's web and get caught in it.

If we do something wrong, or sin, we can expect trouble from our behavior. There is no sense in trying to blame others for our discomfort.

The solution to behavior-caused stress is to change our behavior. If it hurts to hit myself on the hand with a hammer, maybe I should stop doing that.

When we sin, there is often a price to pay. Sin means we crossed over the line from doing good and did wrong. If we do wrong, we often cause trouble for others or for ourselves.

People who want to feel better must do better. Lying, stealing, and cheating are ways to create pain.

When we know we are sinning, we should stop it.

"Come back to your senses as you ought, and stop sinning."

1 Corinthians 15:34

Keep thinking

1. Are you doing something wrong that is causing you pain?
2. Why don't you stop it?

Making a Good Choice

Gray socks or blue socks? It seemed like Carrie could never decide. She spent enough time every morning trying to find a top to go with her jeans. How in the world was she expected to pick out socks that wouldn't make her top look like something she borrowed from her mom?

Why did choices seem so difficult, Carrie often wondered. Last year life had seemed much easier. Adapting to middle school with new teachers, new friends, and so many guys made decision making terribly hard. Every morning Carrie agonized in front of the mirror until she was sometimes late for school.

Decision making is hard for most of us. It may become easier with age and experience, but few of us find it a breeze.

One of life's biggest decisions is a choice we can make while we're young. It helps to get this matter settled so we can make sense out of life. We may have to renew this decision once in a while, but the basic commitment can be made now.

Each of us needs to decide if we are going to follow the Lord or if we are going to try and go it alone. No decision is more important because our choice determines how close we are going to walk with God for the years we have on earth.

God sent his Son, Jesus Christ, to this world to live, to die, and to be resurrected for us. Jesus' sacrifice made it possible for us to be united with our Heavenly Father.

Imagine Jesus building a bridge. The bridge allows us to walk over and be with God both for now and forever. When we make our decision to follow God, we walk across that bridge and become God's people.

Smart people make the decision as soon as possible. They get it taken care of. Teenagers are old enough, intelligent enough, and wise enough to make this choice. Decide now to walk across the bridge that Christ made for us.

In the Old Testament a famous general named Joshua offered a similar choice to his people. He gave them this simple, straightforward plea:

> *"But if serving the Lord seems undesirable to you, then choose for yourselves this day whom you will serve, whether the gods your forefathers served beyond the River, or the gods of the Ammonites, in whose land you are living. But as for me and my household, we will serve the Lord."*
>
> *Joshua 24:15*

Keep thinking

1. Have you made a decision about serving the Lord?
2. Can you name one way you can follow the Lord today?

Too Old for Ghosts

When we were kids we'd sit around campfires and tell ghost stories. We would talk about things that went thump, thump, thump in the night. We'd feel shivers go up and down our spines as we heard about creatures walking through graveyards and mummies stalking the alleys.

Maybe we believed in ghosts and maybe we didn't, but the stories certainly gave us the shakes.

Then came the teen years, and ghost stories lost much of their appeal. Horror films made us slide under the theater seats, but we didn't actually believe them.

Today the ghosts that teens are more likely to be afraid of are called anxieties. Those are the things that make us nervous. They increase our uncertainties and make us terribly apprehensive. Anxieties don't run around in sheets or wrapped in ancient cloth. They don't go boo or give off blood-curdling screams, but that doesn't mean they aren't scary.

Anxieties are the things we are afraid might happen. Some of the most familiar anxieties are:

fear of flunking
fear of being rejected
fear of looking like a klutz
fear of saying something stupid
fear of going blank
fear of dropping a ball
fear of being dressed wrong

There are thousands of anxieties (or teen ghosts) running around. What makes one person anxious may not even bother someone else. One teen feels confident about driving a car while another shakes like a blender. One teen loves computers while another is afraid to push a key.

How many times have we studied for a test and still failed it? Probably not very often. So if we study and remain afraid, our fear has little basis. That's called anxiety.

We speak thousands of sentences every day. How often do we say something stupid? Seldom. The problem is we remember the few dumb things we said and let them haunt us.

Sensible fear is good. Irrational fear is bad. Anxieties are the result of letting irrational fears get out of hand.

The Bible tells us to throw our anxieties over to God. God is willing to take our irrational fears for us. The fear that we will stumble, that we will spit when we talk, that someone will begin screaming at us, those are anxieties. Picture God with a gigantic wagon. Toss your anxieties on God's wagon.

"Cast all your anxiety on him because he cares for you."

1 Peter 5:7

Keep thinking

1. Name one irrational fear that makes you anxious.
2. Have you ever dumped that anxiety on God's huge wagon? Would you like to?

A Deserted Island

The ideal life is not one without pressure. We think it would be great to live by ourselves on a deserted island, eating coconuts, pineapples, and fresh oranges. Often people who live alone like that for a while end up leaving. They long to be with people, accept challenges, and deal with a little stress now and again.

God did a great job of creating us to handle pressure. It's like shock absorbers on a car. A set of great shocks allows us to drive over bumps, potholes, and rocks without feeling too much impact. A shake may be there but not the full force.

If God wanted to, he could remove all stress from our lives. We could wake up each day without a care, without a choice to make, without a risk to take. There are people like that, but most of them live in care homes because they can no longer juggle the pressures of everyday living.

Shuffling the stress of each day is a large part of being alive. From pressure we learn love, strength, grace, hope, peace, ability, adaptability, self-confidence, sacrifice, courage, and other attributes that make us who we are.

Our goal is not to remove all stress. It's far better for us if we find its value.

The apostle Paul told us he chose to apply pressure in his own life. He accepted the challenge to serve God and get involved. That decision was costly.

He was misunderstood, disliked, made fun of, ridiculed, and shunned. Beyond that Paul was also beaten, stoned, hated, and hunted.

The Christian life carries its own pressure. It's a good pressure, one that God calls us to. We aren't invited to become Christians so we can stop living. A large part of following Christ is to live life to its fullest.

God wants us to serve him and serve the people around us. That could be stressful. But it's the kind of stress we are able to handle because God gives us spiritual shock absorbers.

> *"I press on toward the goal to win the prize for which God has called me heavenward in Christ Jesus."*
>
> *Philippians 3:14*

Keep thinking

1. How do you presently serve God?
2. How would you like to serve God?

Carrying a Burden

Snow pasted itself on his glasses. Every few feet he pulled out a handkerchief and wiped them. Tyler thought of how glad he would be when he finally finished shoveling the drive. When the wind shifted to the north, his left ear became clogged with soft wet flakes.

"I wish my parents weren't so cheap," the thirteen-year-old said to himself. "If they'd break down and buy a snowblower, I could do this in no time."

Tyler stopped to shake slush off his shovel. Tap. Tap. He knocked the broad scoop against the pavement to remove clinging snow. He was becoming weary. He appeared to be pausing more than actually shoveling.

Eventually the disgruntled Tyler arrived at the end of the drive. Exhausted, he took the shovel handle in his left hand and headed for the garage.

As Tyler walked toward the garage he could hear a scraping noise. He recognized it immediately. It was the familiar sound of a shovel being pushed against the pavement. He stopped, lowered his glasses, and looked across the street. There he saw Mr. Blumfield bent over, shoveling his walk.

"That's hard work for a man almost eighty," Tyler thought. "I don't know how he does it."

As he began to open the garage door, the teenager heard it again. Scrape. Scrape.

"Time for some hot chocolate," Tyler smiled to himself.

Scrape. Scrape.

He turned his head. Tyler could see snow blowing across the stooped back of his elderly neighbor.

"Oh, what's the dif . . . ?" he said quietly.

Tyler bounded over the piles of snow in the middle of the street. A minute later he was pushing his shovel down Mr. Blumfield's long walk.

All of us have troubles. We have walks to shovel, errands to run, tests to prepare for, and some rude people to try and make happy. It's easy to feel crushed underneath our own burdens.

Often we feel better if we take time to help others with their burdens. For a little while we take our eyes off ourselves and help a friend, a neighbor, a relative. When we lighten someone else's burden, usually our own burden feels lighter, too.

"Help carry one another's burdens, and in this way you will obey the law of Christ."
Galatians 6:2 (TEV)

Keep thinking

1. Who have you helped lately?
2. Who could you help today?

Never Number One

Do you get angry when you don't finish first?
    Do you throw a fit?
    Do you break things?
    Do you get mad at yourself,
    Because you came in second?

Do you cry when your team loses?
    Do you dislike the person who gets top grades?
    Are you upset at the cheerleaders?
    Do you wish you had a car
    Like someone else at school?

When you see others win
    Or receive a prize
    Or get an award
    Or get named first,
    Does that toast you?

Are you ever disgusted with yourself
    Because others make the top of the list
    And you seldom do?

Are you bothered when friends succeed
    And you come in second?
Some of us see life as a contest

    Where everyone is either a winner or a loser.
    That means, in many events,

There is one winner and twelve losers.
If you see life as only winners
And losers,
Life will be miserable.

Instead of trying to beat everyone,
    We need to become humble
    And say it's okay
    When other people win.

We can participate.
    We can give it our best.
    We can train hard.
    We can study long.
    But we need genuine humility.

We need to be happy with ourselves.
    We need to be satisfied with
    Who we are.

We can ask God to give us humility
    So we won't be angry
    When someone else wins.

*"Humble yourselves before the Lord,
and he will lift you up."*

                                    James 4:10

Keep thinking

1. Do you get angry at someone who wins? Why or why not?
2. Are you happy to participate or do you have to win?

Times Get Tough

Some teens face very difficult situations. Most teens encounter more tension than their parents or grandparents did in their teen years. Take this short test and see how much stress there is for you and your friends.

1. What percentage of your friends live in homes of divorce?
2. How many students in your school do you think have a gun or a knife with them or in their lockers?
3. How many teens do you know who have problems because they drink alcohol?
4. Do you know someone with AIDS?
5. How many girls do you know who have been pregnant?
6. How many teens do you know who use drugs other than alcohol?
7. How many parties have you been to where alcohol was consumed by minors?
8. Have you known of a teen who has committed suicide?
9. Have you heard gunfire in your school or neighborhood?
10. How many teens have you known who have been in rehabilitation programs?

The numbers you give for each question will be much higher than most parents would guess. Times are tough today for young people.

This is an important time for teens to turn to Jesus Christ to find strength and guidance. Those who face tough times with a faith in God could find it much easier to cope.

"The troubles of my heart have multiplied; free me from my anguish.
Look upon my affliction and my distress and take away all my sins.
See how my enemies have increased and how fiercely they hate me!
Guard my life and rescue me; let me not be put to shame, for I take refuge in you."
                                    Psalm 25:17-20

Keep thinking

1. Do you feel like you are living in tough times?
2. Have you asked God to help you through these dangers?